# YOUR KNOWLEDGE HAS VALUE

- We will publish your bachelor's and
  master's thesis, essays and papers

- Your own eBook and book -
  sold worldwide in all relevant shops

- Earn money with each sale

Upload your text at www.GRIN.com
and publish for free

**Imprint:**

Copyright © 2014 GRIN Verlag, Open Publishing GmbH
Print and binding: Books on Demand GmbH, Norderstedt Germany
ISBN: 9783656825333


**This book at GRIN:**

http://www.grin.com/en/e-book/283267/arcade-as-japanese-traditional-shopping-and-business-culture

Kazutaka Hashimoto

# Arcade as Japanese Traditional Shopping and Business Culture

GRIN Publishing

# Arcade as Japanese Traditional Shopping and Business Culture

Kazutaka HASHIMOTO

Kanto Gakuin University,

Yokohama, Japan

## Introduction

This paper will examine the roles and meanings of arcades in Japan. The so-called arcade, to some extent resembles the roofed galleries （騎廊） and shophouses （騎楼） that exist in East Asia and Southeast Asia. In Taiwan, roofed galleries are characterized by a continuous pavement and are known as *Tingtsuzao* （亭仔脚）. In Japan, there are not any shophouses, however there are roofed galleries in which European style store fronts (*passages*) are a common feature. The style that covered a shopping street with an arcade has been usual for a business revitalization in Japan. That is, Japanese arcades were developed with the intention of revitalizing the economy. Such arcades also, happily, facilitate easy human relationships between merchants, sales personnel and customers. The paper considers the revitalizations and its realities of the shopping streets in Japanese inner-city, through showing the realities of many Japan's shopping arcades.

<u>Roofed galleries and Shophouses</u>

Roofed galleries exist in the Philippines, Vietnam as well as Taiwan. *Tingtsuzao* in Taiwan were initially introduced as a way of urban renewals by Japanese colonial administrators. In the 1910s, cholera, typhoid, and the plague spread in Taiwan. Streets were narrow and street drains polluted the cities. After 1912, urban renewal projects were carried out in order to widen streets and build sewerage systems. Tingtsuzao were set, instead, because the front areas of buildings were removed (Aoi 2005 211).

Roofed galleries in the Philippines' were founded in Bacold and Sillay, Negros Island. Roofed galleries designed in a distinct Spanish style construction are located in Sillay, although one of the two is newer as it was built in 1908: a typical opulent house characteristic of those seen at the turn of the 20th century. Also, in Vietnam, roofed galleries exist in Ho Chi Minh City and Hanoi. In Ho Chi Minh City, the roofed gallery area of the national department store in Nguyen Hue Street has been cleaned, however, motorbikes and goods can be found under the roofed galleries around Ben Tanh Market. Also, the Hotel Continental Saigon has a roofed gallery, and the history of the roofed gallery is surprisingly long as the French style hotel was constructed in 1880. In Hanoi, Trang Tien street is also the location of roofed galleries. In particular, there is the roofed gallery of Trang Tien Plaza which extends along the street.

In Singapore and Malaysia, shophouses can be found in many places. I observed shophouses in Ipoh, Penang, Johor Bahru and Mersing in Malaysia, in addition to Little India, Chinatown, Arab Street and Singapore riverside in Singapore. Most of the shophouses in Trader Markets located along the Singapore riverside were constructed before the mid-1880s.

The shophouse styles were adopted from southern China. David G. Kohl states, "Villages in rural Kwangtung are often walled, and houses within the community share common party walls. Corridor-type villages are arranged with terrace houses built in two or more parallel rows, separated by narrow lanes between the rows of houses. A third type of village arrangement places houses in rows along roadways. In all cases, the houses are connected with a shared party wall, which bears the weight of the purlins and the single or double-tiled roof." (Kohl 1984: 172) In addition to the description of villages as outlined by Kohl, I would add that the construction design ideas originated from the corridors of Chinese temples and furthermore, the eaves or tents of shops.

In Singapore, Stamford Raffles (1922) instructed that all houses built with brick or tile should have a uniform type of front, and "each house should have a verandah of a certain depth open at all times as a continued and covered passage on each side of the street" (Kohl 1984: 157, Yeoh 1996: 245). This design format was introduced in 5 foot ways in the roofed galleries in Singapore and the Strait Settlements.


Arcades in Japan

1. Origin of the Arcade in Japan

In 2009,   the number of shopping streets covered entirely with an arcade in Japan totalled over 573. The city of Osaka, with a total of 70, has the highest number of arcades in Japan. The second highest number of arcades can be found in the 23 wards of Tokyo with the number totalling 34. The third is Kobe City with the number of arcades numbered at 29. Osaka has the longest arcade in Japan: Tenjinbashi Suji, which is 2.6 kilometers in length.

The shopping arcade regarded as the oldest is named Uomachi Ginten Gai, Kokura, Kita Kyushu and dates back to 1951. However, the Takegawara Koji Arcade located in Beppu may in fact be the oldest Japanese arcade as it was already constructed in 1921. The arcade was constructed in order to prevent Beppu Spa's guests from getting their yukatas wet when it rained. The overhead of Takegawara Koji Arcade was covered with glass and resembled a street in Canton as described by Kohl. However, the overhead construction of the street in Canton featured bamboo slats for protection from the sun (Kohl 1984: 174).

*http://www.beppers.jp/takegawara/newpage1.html*

The history of roofed galleries in Japan is older than the European style arcades seen in Japan. In Kuroishi City, Aormori Prefecture, merchant houses constructed with *Komise* (roofed galleries) during the Edo period (1716-1735) were designed to provide shelter from the snow. In Niigata, roofed galleries developed from Gangi, were designed in order to provide shelter from the snow, and can be seen on both sides of the mainstreet.

2. Purpose of the Construction of Shopping Arcades

An arcade is constructed for the purpose of increasing the number of customers to an area through creating a lively shopping street atmosphere. Prior to the 1990s, arcades functioned to provide shelter from the rain or snow, for protection from the sun, and for closing the area to cars. In addition, arcades contribute to maintaining the quality of goods. For example, in Kawasaki Ginryugai, an arcade that was constructed with stained glass was established in 1980. The arcade construction was carried out at a total cost of 450 million yen and was designed to create a deluxe shopping street where customers could enjoy shopping. During the summer season every year, Ginryugai celebrates *tanabata matsuri* (the star festival). In 2009, premium gift certificates were sold to celebrate the 60 year anniversary of the establishment of the arcade. Furthermore, *Tanabata matsuri* is famous in Sendai with Chuo Dori Shotengai the main street where the festival is conducted. The street, measuring 800 meters in length, is a wide, modernized and fashionable area. On rainy days, the arcade brings customers into the shopping street (Takahashi 2007: 24).

*by author*

In order to upgrade the amenities for customers, Kohama Shotengai, Osaka, renewed the old arcade and the colored paved street from 1999-2000. Subsequently, Kohama Shotengai was selected as "Ganbaru Shotengai 77"(Best effort for a shopping street out of 77 areas) by the Japanese Small and Medium Enterprises Agency. Kohama Shotengai is situated at the approach to Sumiyoshi Taisha (shrine): in the New Year of 2009, visitors numbered 2.35 million, and on the first Dragon day (based on the twelve horary signs) in every month visitors number 10 thousand. The shopping street has achieved success by means of holding a fair on the first

Dragon day. In this type of way, Japanese arcades have contributed to revitalizing the local economy.


Arcade as a Space for Developing Positive Human Relationships

The construction of an arcade involves an enormous financial cost as can be seen in the case of Kawasaki Ginryugai. Therefore, many storekeeper's associations have relied on government funds. For example, in recent years the Japanese Government has offered subsidies in order to support the revitalization of central urban districts. The storekeeper's associations have used these loans in order to modernize or upgrade shopping streets. The use and return of loans by storekeeper's associations require power, strong will, business ability and cohesion. Generally though, there is a degree of rivalry and jealousy that exists between shops, and this results in the decrease in cohesion within a storekeeper's association and a shopping street. So, it is important that a storekeeper's association and a shopping street work together to strengthen their cohesion and cooperation. It follows that the arcade functions as a venue for the development of human relationships between storekeepers.

In addition, human relationships between customers and the shops grow to become much more than just simple acquaintances. This is the result of customers repeatedly purchasing goods at shops in an arcade. On April 27th 2007, Hama Market, Isogo Ward, Yokohama was set on fire and was partially

*by author*

6

destroyed (as shown the right photo). A local guitarist, Shinozaki Yoko, wrote a song in order to uplift the community and express hope for the reconstruction of Hama Market. Shinozaki has been a frequent visitor to the arcade over a period of about 20 years and points out that she enjoys the warm human relationships that exist between customers and shops.


<u>Risks Faced by Shopping Arcades and the Process of Removal</u>

As discussed earlier in this paper, arcades are constructed firstly for the purpose of increasing customers to an area through the construction of a lively shopping street. Second, an arcade functions to provide shelter from rain or snow, for protection from the sun and for closing an area to traffic such as cars. Third, arcades contribute to the maintenance and the quality of goods. Fourth, arcades encourage customers and shops to establish relationships that are more than just acquaintances.

However, when old shopping arcades fall into disrepair and are not renovated, the atmosphere can soon become dark. In particular, if the number of customers decreases and shops are forced to pull down their shutters, the result is that dark air rapidly fills the area. Lights are partly turned off due to the increase in closed shops within an arcade. Also, ceiling lights are partly turned off for economical reasons. Dusty arcades become dark. The shopping arcade joining Kokudo station of JR Tsurumi Line is an example of a dying arcade. Furthermore, there are some old shopping arcades in Osaka. Established in 1957, the arcade of Tsuruhashi Hondori Shotenkai is an old shopping street. While the long shopping arcade has a dark atmosphere and many closed shops can be seen, it nevertheless seems to be alive in the neighborhood as it serves as a traditional shopping street.

Fifty-three storekeeper's associations out of 55 local cities associations in Japan have indicated that they would like to reinvigerate their old shopping arcades. Thirty-two associations want to improve their arcades, and 20 associations want removal of the covered roof structure. In the case of arcades that were constructed over 20 years ago, 17 out of 40 arcades have indicated that they want the removal of the roof structure. Arcade roof structure removals started from the 1990s. Isezaki-cho, Yokohama, had been a representative shopping street since pre-World War II Japan. Isezaki Mall Shopping Street was formerly the location of a shopping arcade, and was remodelled as an uncovered mall street arcade in 1978. It was designed as a tree-lined street and telegraph poles were taken away in order to revive the feeling of an old-style shopping street. The street includes such features as street furniture and sculptures, in addition to attractive pasted tiles. The floor area covers 60,000 square meters, and the annual sales of the retail shops were calculated to be 60 billion yen in 1977, and these figures have continued to soar due to the mall. Nevertheless, the shopping street has not been overly prosperous, as can be seen in the closure of the Yokohama Matsuzakaya Department store in 2008 (Hashimoto 2009a).

Odori shopping street, the main street of Utsunomiya, Tochigi Prefecture had a roofed gallery built before the 1990s, however the Utsunomiya  city hall has promoted its removal. It is regrettable that old and unattractive roofed galleries still remain covering  the street. Utsunomiya Landscape Planning (2007) noted that the roofed gallery would be removed, however Utsunomiya remains an unsuccessful case of the removal of an arcade (Hashimoto 2009b).

<u>Conclusion</u>

Japan's shopping arcades constitute a traditional culture in the inner-city. That is to say, they are the home for traditional business culture, landscape, business practices, and the human relationships that are formed. The Japanese arcades have contributed significantly to the revitalization of the economy, as discussed above.

However, old shopping arcades that have been unable to Cohesion and cooperation between storekeepers, in addition to sufficient funds, are necessary for the removal or improvement of shopping arcades. And even then, the effort of storekeepers in order to promote business vitalization has limits, because an arcade will always face competition from other shopping streets, supermarkets and department stores. City planning as well as the support for shopping streets from local governments are the keys to success. A question of vital importance for shopping streets is how local governments can contribute to city planning in order to promote business revitalization.

*Note:*

*This paper was published at first in The electronic proceedings for the Second International Conference of the Japanese Studies Association in Southeast Asia (2009).*

References:

Aoi,   A. (2005)"Toshi no Hifu"(Urban Skin: Urban History and Shophouses in Taiwan), *Asia Yugaku*, No. 80.

Hashimoto, K. (2009a) "Understanding Shitamachi in Yokohama,"*Asian Profile*, Vol. 37, No.3.

Hashimoto, K. (2009b) "The Sociology of Arcade," K. Hashimoto, H. Fujita and N. Yoshihara, eds. *Urban Social Planning o Kanagaeru* (Considering of Urban Social Planning), Toshindo, Tokyo.

Kohl, D. G. (1984) *Chinese Architecture in the Straits Settlements and Western Malaya: Temples, Kongsis and Houses*, Heineman Asia, Kuala Lumpur.

Nakajima, R. (2008) "Chiho Toshi no Chushin Shigaichi Shotengai niokeru Zengaishiki Arcade Tekkyo no Doko to Jittai ni kansuru Kenkyu" (A Study on the Trend and Details of the Removal of Covered Arcades in Downtown Shopping Street in Local Cities) , *43th Conference in Nippon Toshi Keikaku Gakkai.*

Takahashi, H. (2007)    *Toshi to Shohi Shakai tono Deai* (The Encounter between City and Consumption Societies), Ochanomizu Shobo, Tokyo.

Yeoh, B. S. A. (1996) *Contesting Space: Power Relations and the Urban Built Environment in Colonial Singapore*, Oxford, New York.